# WEATHER AND NATURAL DISASTERS

**MELISSA RAÉ SHOFNER**

## PowerKiDS press

NEW YORK

Published in 2017 by The Rosen Publishing Group, Inc.
29 East 21st Street, New York, NY 10010

Editor: Melissa Raé Shofner
Book Design: Michael Flynn
Interior Layout: Mickey Harmon

Photo Credits: Cover (image) solarseven/Shutterstock.com; p. 4 tea maeklong/Shutterstock.com; p. 5 (snow) Skylines/Shutterstock.com; p. 5 (rain) peresanz/Shutterstock.com; p. 5 (main) Minerva Studio/Shutterstock.com; p. 7 Harvepino/Shutterstock.com; p. 9 (hail) Ryszard Stelmachowicz/Shutterstock.com; p. 9 (main) Vasin Lee/Shutterstock.com; p. 10 EmiliaUngar/Shutterstock.com; p. 11 https://commons.wikimedia.org/wiki/File:Hurricane_isabel2_2003.jpg; p. 12 sunsinger/Shutterstock.com; p. 13 montree hanlue/Shutterstock.com; p. 15 (main) Ipedan/Shutterstock.com; p. 15 (inset) Handout/Handout/Getty Images News/Getty Images; p. 16 InterNetwork Media/Getty Images; p. 17 Leemage/Contributor/Universal Images Group/Getty Images; p. 19 Elnur/Shutterstock.com; p. 20 Vladimir Melnikov/Shutterstock.com; p. 21 Ethan Miller/Staff/Getty Images News/Getty Images; p. 22 Joe Raedle/Staff/Getty Images News/Getty Images.

Cataloging-in-Publication Data
Names: Shofner, Melissa Raé.
Title: Weather and natural disasters / Melissa Raé Shofner.
Description: New York : PowerKids Press, 2017. | Series: Spotlight on earth science | Includes index.
Identifiers: ISBN 9781499425475 (pbk.) | ISBN 9781499425505 (library bound) | ISBN 9781499425482 (6 pack)
Subjects: LCSH: Weather--Juvenile literature. | Natural disasters--Juvenile literature.
Classification: LCC QC981.3 S56 2017 | DDC 551.5--dc23

Manufactured in the United States of America

CPSIA Compliance Information: Batch #BW17PK For further information contact Rosen Publishing, New York, New York at 1-800-237-9932.

# CONTENTS

WHAT IS WEATHER? . . . . . . . . . . . . . . . . . . . . . . . . . . 4

WHAT ARE NATURAL DISASTERS? . . . . . . . . . . . . . . . 6

SUPERSTORMS . . . . . . . . . . . . . . . . . . . . . . . . . . . . . 8

WILD WINDS . . . . . . . . . . . . . . . . . . . . . . . . . . . . . .10

HOT AND DRY . . . . . . . . . . . . . . . . . . . . . . . . . . . . .12

BLIZZARDS . . . . . . . . . . . . . . . . . . . . . . . . . . . . . . .14

WHEN THE EARTH MOVES . . . . . . . . . . . . . . . . . . . .16

SLIDING AWAY . . . . . . . . . . . . . . . . . . . . . . . . . . . . .18

WILDFIRES . . . . . . . . . . . . . . . . . . . . . . . . . . . . . . . 20

ADVANCES IN TECHNOLOGY . . . . . . . . . . . . . . . . . .22

GLOSSARY . . . . . . . . . . . . . . . . . . . . . . . . . . . . . . .23

INDEX . . . . . . . . . . . . . . . . . . . . . . . . . . . . . . . . . . 24

PRIMARY SOURCE LIST . . . . . . . . . . . . . . . . . . . . . 24

WEBSITES . . . . . . . . . . . . . . . . . . . . . . . . . . . . . . . 24

# CHAPTER ONE

# WHAT IS WEATHER?

What is the weather like where you live? Does it rain a lot, or is it sunny most of the year? Do you get snow in winter? Do you live in an area that is very windy?

Weather is the state of the atmosphere, or the mixture of gases around a planet, at any given time. It could be sunny, windy, rainy, or snowy. Everyone knows the weather doesn't stay the same as time changes. The morning could be rainy, and the afternoon could be sunny. The behavior of weather over a longer period of time in a given area is known as climate.

Weather events are caused by the sun and Earth's atmosphere. Scientists called meteorologists study numerous elements of Earth's atmosphere, including temperature, **precipitation**, cloudiness, wind, and **atmospheric pressure**. By monitoring these elements, meteorologists can make better forecasts. New technology has allowed them to do this.

A cricket's chirping varies according to the outside temperature. If you count the number of times a cricket chirps in 14 seconds and then add 40, the resulting number will be the approximate temperature in degrees Fahrenheit.

**SNOW**

**RAIN**

# CHAPTER TWO

# WHAT ARE NATURAL DISASTERS?

Depending where on Earth you live, you can experience many different kinds of weather during a year. Some areas, such as south Florida, are well known for hot, sunny days year round. This makes them ideal places to vacation, even in winter. However, Florida and other areas are also well known for hurricanes part of the year.

Hurricanes are just one kind of natural disaster. Others include tornadoes, blizzards, and mudslides. Some natural disasters, such as earthquakes and volcanic eruptions, aren't a direct result of weather events. Natural disasters often result in the loss of life and property.

Luckily for us, many trained scientists watch Earth for signs of natural disasters. However, scientists can't be 100 percent correct all the time. Some natural disasters, such as earthquakes, can't be **predicted** at all. That's when severe weather and natural disasters can be most harmful to people.

Hurricanes are more likely to happen during certain times of the year. The Atlantic hurricane season occurs from June 1 to November 30, but hurricanes are more likely in the fall months. The Eastern Pacific hurricane season is May 15 to November 30.

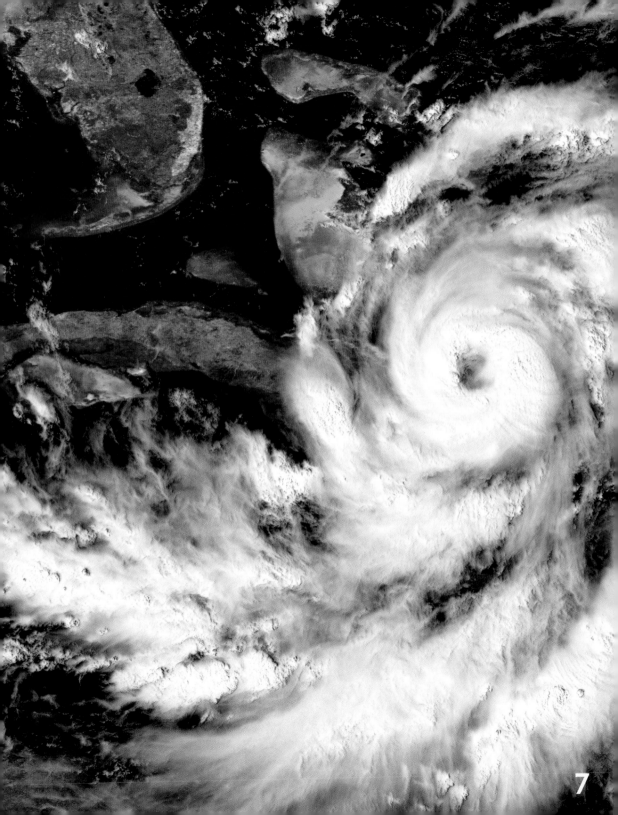

# CHAPTER THREE

# SUPERSTORMS

Most people on Earth are familiar with thunderstorms. A thunderstorm is a rain shower when thunder can be heard and lightning can be seen. At any moment, Earth is experiencing 2,000 thunderstorms. There are an estimated 16 million thunderstorms each year.

Thunderstorms form when **convection currents** in the atmosphere cause warm air to rise. Water vapor in the air cools and forms clouds. As this process continues, ice **particles** in the atmosphere rub together and form an electric charge in the cloud. In time, the charge is released, or let go, in the form of lightning. This release of electricity creates sound waves that we hear as thunder.

A severe thunderstorm is one accompanied by strong winds, which can result in a tornado. Severe thunderstorms may also drop hail. Sometimes a storm drops rain so quickly flooding occurs.

The sun's surface is hot, but a lightning strike is much hotter. The surface of the sun is about 10,000° Fahrenheit (5,538° Celsius). Lightning heats the air around it to more than 50,000° Fahrenheit (27,760° Celsius) in just a fraction of a second!

# HAIL

# CHAPTER FOUR

# WILD WINDS

The wind may feel nice when it's just a breeze, but it can become very powerful. Hurricanes and tornadoes both include winds that can cause a lot of **damage**.

| ENHANCED FUJITA SCALE |
| --- |
| EF5 +200 MPH |
| EF4 166–200 MPH |
| EF3 136–165 MPH |
| EF2 111–135 MPH |
| EF1 86–110 MPH |
| EF0 65–85 MPH |

Tornadoes in the United States are now rated using the Enhanced Fujita Scale. The scale rates the intensity, or power, of tornadoes based on damage caused. This scale replaces the original Fujita Scale, which rated tornadoes based on tornado wind speeds that weren't scientifically proven.

HURRICANE ISABEL
SEPTEMBER 14, 2003

Hurricanes and tornadoes are very similar. A hurricane is a huge, spinning storm that forms over the ocean and creates lots of rain. These storms have strong winds and can cause high waves on the ocean and flooding on land. These floods are called storm surges. A tornado is air that spins very fast in a circle and is touching both the ground and a cloud.

# CHAPTER FIVE

# HOT AND DRY

It's expected that summers in most parts of the world will be hot, but over time the weather has become much hotter and much drier.

The Patagonian desert in South America is arid, or very dry. Very little plant life exists here, but there is some, such as the few bushes shown here.

Droughts are usually the result of several causes at once, including global weather patterns and areas of high pressure. This makes them hard for meteorologists to predict.

Many places experience heat waves, or times when the temperature is higher than it normally is. Heat waves have been linked to global warming and can cause problems for animal and human populations.

Heat waves can result in droughts. A drought is when there's very little precipitation over a period of time. Sometimes droughts develop quickly and last a short time. Other times, droughts develop slowly and last several years. In some parts of the world, dry conditions in which animals don't live and plants don't grow are perfectly normal. These places are called deserts.

# CHAPTER SIX

# BLIZZARDS

There may be blizzards in places where it snows. Some people think that snow is all it takes to make a blizzard, but these storms involve much more. A blizzard is a type of severe snowstorm that has strong winds and blowing or falling snow. These conditions must last for at least three hours.

Different types of blizzards have different causes. Some blizzards happen when it isn't snowing but the wind picks up snow that has already fallen. This is called a ground blizzard. Sometimes, blizzards are a result of strong winds coming from the northern Atlantic Ocean. These blizzards are known as Nor'easters.

Blizzards may create very unsafe conditions. **Whiteouts** are times of low visibility due to snow. This means it's very hard to see or be seen. During a whiteout, people can get lost while walking, and sometimes car accidents happen. People can get **hypothermia** from being outside during a blizzard.

Blizzards make it very hard to see your surroundings. In order to be called a blizzard, a storm must have winds of 35 miles (56.3 km) per hour or more and visibility of less than a quarter mile (0.4 km).

Meteorologists use satellite images to see storms from space. This image shows areas of high atmospheric moisture during a severe winter storm in 2011.

# CHAPTER SEVEN

# WHEN THE EARTH MOVES

Sometimes, natural disasters aren't caused by weather systems. Shifting **tectonic plates** may cause earthquakes. The shifting usually occurs along a fault line, which is the place where two pieces of Earth's crust meet.

Volcanic eruptions may also cause earthquakes. These earthquakes are usually weaker than those caused by tectonic plates. When one plate slides under another, **molten** rock known as magma is released and rises to the surface.

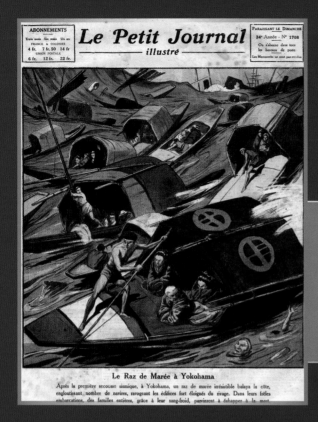

**Le Petit Journal illustré**

ABONNEMENTS
Trois mois 5m mois Un an
FRANCE & COLONIES
4 fr.  7 fr. 50  14 fr
UNION POSTALE
6 fr.  12 fr.  22 fr.

PARAISSANT LE DIMANCHE
34ᵉ Année · N° 1708

Le Raz de Marée à Yokohama

Après la première secousse sismique, à Yokohama, un raz de marée irrésistible balaya la côte, engloutissant nombre de navires, ravageant les édifices fort éloignés du rivage. Dans leurs frêles embarcations, des familles entières, grâce à leur sang-froid, parvinrent à échapper à la mort.

This French newspaper from September 16, 1923, features a drawing of boats caught in the tsunami caused by the 1923 Great Kanto earthquake in Yokohama, Japan.

If an earthquake begins in the earth underneath the ocean, it may result in a tsunami, or large ocean wave. Tsunamis are very hard to predict and often cause a lot of damage to coastal cities. When a tsunami starts in the deep ocean, the wave may be fairly weak by the time it reaches the coast. If a tsunami begins closer to the coastline, entire cities may be destroyed.

On March 20, 1980, the area around Mount Saint Helens—a volcano in southwestern Washington—experienced a magnitude 4.2 earthquake. After weeks of earthquake activity, the volcano erupted on May 18, 1980. Mount Saint Helens hadn't been active in 123 years!

# CHAPTER EIGHT

# SLIDING AWAY

Weather has the ability to cause the land and snow to become loosened. This creates unsafe conditions. Two of the most common types of shifting land are mudslides and landslides.

Landslides sometimes happen after an earthquake when large rocks and dirt are released from a higher elevation, or height above sea level. They can also be caused by human activity. Mudslides are similar to landslides and occur when rivers of rock and mud move down a slope. Mudslides are usually caused by heavy rain, but they may also be caused by things like construction and **erosion**.

The loosening of snow on a mountainside may lead to an avalanche. Avalanches sometimes occur when a person or animal unsettles the snow. This may cause a large section of snow or ice to break free. Avalanches of thick, packed snow result in much more damage than avalanches of light, powdery snow.

It's very important to be careful when skiing or snowboarding. Avalanches may happen without warning at any time. People unsettling sections of snow cause most avalanches.

# CHAPTER NINE

# WILDFIRES

Do people cause wildfires or does the weather? Wildfires may actually be caused by both, but they're connected to dry plant life and strong winds. Wildfires can start if a person drops a match or a car releases a spark. They can also be caused naturally by lightning strikes. Global warming has added to the number of wildfires that occur each year because droughts cause plant life to dry up.

Although wildfires burn very rapidly and can destroy entire forests, they're not all bad. Wildfires are actually very important for nature's growth cycle because they add **nutrients** back into the soil by burning plants. Wildfires also ensure that sick plants don't make other plants in an area ill. After a wildfire occurs in a very thick forest, sunlight can reach the forest floor and allow new trees to grow.

Four out of five wildfires are caused by people. Smokey Bear has been helping prevent wildfires since 1944.

FIRE DANGER

HIGH

TODAY !

PREVENT FOREST FIRES

# CHAPTER TEN

# ADVANCES IN TECHNOLOGY

Can you imagine a time when it was nearly impossible to predict the weather in advance? This would make it even harder for you to prepare for a natural disaster. Thankfully, modern **technology** has made it much easier to see possible changes in weather before they occur. This makes it easier for meteorologists to advise people about the weather for the next few days. Improvements to existing technologies also help people predict weather patterns sooner. This allows people to make educated safety decisions. Most natural disasters are also easier to predict thanks to modern technology.

Many of the advances in weather-predicting technology are due to the need for better training for forecasters. Forecasters are able to read data more accurately than before, which also helps them give people enough warning to stay safe in instances of severe weather.

# GLOSSARY

**atmospheric pressure** (at-muh-SFEER-ihk PREH-shur)  The pressure exerted in every direction at any given point by the weight of the atmosphere.

**convection current** (kuhn-VEK-shun KUHR-uhnt)  The transfer of heat by the movement in a gas or liquid in which the warmer parts move up and the colder parts move down.

**damage** (DAA-mij)  Loss or harm done to a person or piece of property.

**erosion** (ih-ROH-zhun)  The wearing away of Earth's surface by wind or water.

**hypothermia** (hy-puh-THUR-mee-uh)  Dangerously low body temperature caused by cold conditions.

**molten** (MOL-tuhn)  Made liquid by heat.

**nutrient** (NOO-tree-uhnt)  Something taken in by a plant or animal that helps it grow and stay healthy.

**particle** (PAR-tih-kuhl)  A small piece of matter.

**precipitation** (preh-sih-puh-TAY-shun)  Water that falls to the ground as hail, mist, rain, sleet, or snow.

**predict** (prih-DIKT)  To guess what will happen in the future based on facts or knowledge.

**technology** (tek-NAH-luh-jee)  A method that uses science to solve problems and the tools used to solve those problems.

**tectonic plate** (tehk-TAH-nihk PLAYT)  One of the moveable masses of rock that make up Earth's surface.

**whiteout** (WYT-owt)  A condition in which falling or blowing snow makes visibility very poor.

# INDEX

**A**
atmosphere, 4, 8
avalanche, 18, 19

**B**
blizzard, 6, 14

**C**
climate, 4

**D**
drought, 13, 20

**E**
earthquake, 6, 16, 18
Enhanced Fujita Scale, 10

**F**
flooding, 8, 11
Florida, 6

**G**
global warming, 13, 20

**H**
hail, 8, 9
heat wave, 13
hurricane, 6, 10, 11

**L**
landslide, 18
lightning, 8, 20

**M**
meteorologist, 4, 13, 22
Mount Saint Helens, 16
mudslide, 6, 18

**N**
Nor'easter, 14

**P**
precipitation, 4, 13

**R**
rain, 4, 5, 8, 11, 18

**S**
snow, 4, 5, 14, 18, 19
South America, 12
storm surge, 11

**T**
temperature, 4, 13
thunder, 8
thunderstorm, 8
tornado, 6, 8, 10, 11
tsunami, 16, 17

**V**
volcanic eruption, 6, 16

**W**
Washington, 16
whiteout, 14
wildfire, 20, 21
wind, 4, 8, 10, 11, 14, 20

# PRIMARY SOURCE LIST

**Page 11**
Hurricane Isabel. Satellite image. September 14, 2003. By Jacques Descloitres, MODIS Rapid Response Team, NASA/GSFC.

**Page 15**
High atmospheric moisture, shown in blue, of a severe winter storm. Satellite image. January 31, 2011. From NASA/NOAA GOES project.

**Page 17**
Boats in tsunami caused by 1923 Great Kanto earthquake in Yokohama, Japan. Drawing. September 16, 1923. Front page of *Le Petite Journal*, France.

# WEBSITES

Due to the changing nature of Internet links, PowerKids Press has developed an online list of websites related to the subject of this book. This site is updated regularly. Please use this link to access the list: www.powerkidslinks.com/soes/wnd